AF220250

Will our love survive, or do I

let fate decide?

LUCA GOMES

Will our love survive, or do I let fate decide?

Luca Gomes

Bibliografische Information der Deutschen Nationalbibliothek: Die Deutsche Nationalbibliothek verzeichnet diese Publikation in der Deutschen Nationalbibliografie; detaillierte bibliografische Daten sind im Internet über dnb.dnb.de abrufbar.

Herstellung und Verlag: BoD – Books on Demand, Norderstedt

ISBN: 978-3-7562-3368-7

Will Our Love Survive Or Do I Let Fate Decide?

Heaven To Hell Guide

This book is filled with
thoughts that follow me
through the light of day and the
dawn of night.
I guess you can call it my
therapy.

–Purpose

Heavenly

We often get so caught up in our sad and scary thoughts, that we forget the beauty of life, that is happening right in front of us.

In those times it is especially difficult, to see life as it is and the beauty that hides behind most situations.

We need to make the most of what we've got and handle life accordingly. Don't let negative thoughts take your joy of life, find new ways to make it enjoyable again!

- *Luca Gomes*

"The law is, that every beginning
must come to an end. Your birth
ends with your death, what is in
between calls itself „life".
We need to acknowledge our
existence and that we are currently in
the state of living. Death is closure,
not something to work towards. Live
your life, don't wait for life to live
you."

– *Luca Gomes*

"Autumn.

Radiant leaves, with the shape of perfection.

Love never distant, far away from neglection.

Flowing in the wind, I have met my flower.

Hoping that our feelings might never devour.

I am the hummingbird; on your pollen I feast.

Thy making me wonder, will thy ever leave?

Hopelessly in love.

Scared to get lost.

Staying with you, no matter the cost."

– *Luca Gomes*

"In miserable thought, greatness can
be achieved."

– *Luca Gomes*

"Happiness, I seek
Happiness, I need
Happiness will flee
Until happiness I see
Then and there I Fall to knees
My happiness shall never leave
You and I result in peace."

– Luca Gomes

,,And when you truly accept the fate that has been coming for you all along, you will find total peace in the misery, that now calls itself life."

– *Luca Gomes*

"Lonely days feel grey and empty, until we finally meet again and be truly happy."

– *Luca Gomes*

"I realized that when you really love someone, you don't want to engage in a relationship just so you have this official and special bond, or out of a feeling. You want to do it, to ensure that they don't plan on leaving so easily.

With that I also realized, that love is not a random feeling of butterflies when you see someone, it's when you only want to lay your eyes on that one person and everything else becomes less important. Love makes you not want to chase other people but give all your heart to that one person. Now love can appear physically but reaches its highest value when it's mentally."

– *Luca Gomes*

"I want to be great at what I do, and

if living is what I do,

I want to be great at life."

– *Luca Gomes*

"Life is too beautiful, to enjoy death."

– *Luca Gomes*

"Spend your energy on people who deserve it, forbid yourself to spend it on people who wouldn't even care to return it."

– *Luca Gomes*

"Someday there will come a person
into your life, that completely turns
your world upside down, without
causing any damages."

– *Luca Gomes*

"A blank page. The safe place of my chaotic thoughts."

– *Luca Gomes*

"Is it too fast, or is it really just love?"

– *Luca Gomes*

"Love doesn't just involve happiness, easiness and secureness, it also involves second guessing, worrying, and fighting. It is not about how it comes, it's about what you make of it."

– *Luca Gomes*

"Structures of words behold my sensory. My love falls out, into infinity."

– *Luca Gomes*

"Vibrations gently touch my ear.

Impulses to my brain, making me feel.

Answers find their way to my cognition.

Will it be unity or division?

– Music, my daily therapist."

– *Luca Gomes*

"You are my sunshine and my
delight.

You make me feel so beautiful inside.

Some days are difficult, and some are
fine.

I am so grateful, to call you mine."

– *Luca Gomes*

In Between

,,It is not the temporary pain that one
has to suffer.
It is the consequence of disturbance,
that will follow you into the
brightness of your mind, dimming
your perception of what is truly
beautiful in life."
– *Luca Gomes*

"A bizarre little person, as small as a
berry hanging from the biggest tree
in the forest.
Hanging on a branch with all its
internal power.
Hopes and Dreams resemble the
seasons.
It is then, when the autumn colors
have passed, that the berry will fall to
its destiny with the possibility of
being crushed by the sheer impact of
life."

– *Luca Gomes*

"I for too long have condoned the behaviourism of making bad decisions."

– *Luca Gomes*

"Being different is the confusion of being normal."

– *Luca Gomes*

„She's asking herself what's wrong,

but she never gets the answer right."

– *Luca Gomes*

"You can either see reality or trust uncertainty."

– *Luca Gomes*

"Arguments and questions –

Arguments where we neglect the

entire certainty of the situation.

We need to see the reality as a whole.

Motivations and ambitions.

Prior and in full presence.

How did one change? When did one

change?

Has one changed at all?

What's the need? Is there even a need

at all?

Is it just a simple situation or is it

more than that?

Reasoning is the fulfilled action of
presenting ambition and motivation.
Thus, motives are important in
argumentations and borders.
A person's motives are partly
controlled by actions and character
traits from the past and partly from
the present.
Past and presence are worthy to each
other."

– *Luca Gomes*

„Accepting but not understanding –
the act of going along with it, but
fundamentally disagreeing with what
one has said."

– *Luca Gomes*

,,It's hard to not be understood as different, when you cannot identify with the majority around you."

– *Luca Gomes*

"Egoistic people will never think about how their actions make you feel and therefore not care about the consequences."

– *Luca Gomes*

"Is it even that good, when you regret doing too much, because you're scared that that person now holds an expectation? "

– *Luca Gomes*

"Overthinking is the killer of all joy

and the preparation of all evil."

-Luca Gomes

"Involuntary suffering will lead you to the neglection of positive thought."

– *Luca Gomes*

"We don't want what we can't have,
we want to experience the illusion of
what it could have been."

– *Luca Gomes*

"Sometimes it is the pure lack of will,

that denies our potential."

– *Luca Gomes*

"Everything in life is as certain as the expiry of every beginning."

– *Luca Gomes*

"What makes me special?

At least not the obvious."

– *Luca Gomes*

"One who dares not to be selfish at best, is selfish nonetheless."

– *Luca Gomes*

"Never knew karma would hit me
the way it did.

Never knew it would make my feel
like shit.

But I guess, I won't separate myself
from it.

It's the receipt I get, for the things I
did."

– *Luca Gomes*

"'L'o'V'e and 'H'o'P'e are only separated by two letters."

– *Luca Gomes*

Hell

Sometimes we meet new people and immediately paint a picture of them in our heads. That is called wishful thinking.. Most of the times people won't live up to our expectations and that can be quite hard to accept. Now, you get attached and all of a sudden your picture gets distorted, and you feel like you don't recognize that person anymore. You stay up thinking about the craziest things while the other doesn't think at all. Eventually you must put up with involuntary suffering, wishing for your partner to think about how you're feeling instead of just trying to get their way. What exactly is it, that we are supposed to do at this point? I have yet to find an answer to that.

„Delightfulness seeks itself in suffering. Consequences of attachments and attention. The one who is at thought and the other who stays at neglection. The eeriness of self-suffocating thoughts."

– *Luca Gomes*

"I used to be your soulmate, now I'm just an unknown visitor in your ghost town of remembrance."

– *Luca Gomes*

"Disparity –

Blue Greatness.

Darkness of the abyss.

Clouded by my foggy breath, that
fills the horizon.

My heart resonating with the water I
am surrounded by.

Neighboured by great nothingness, I
feel my body getting weak.

My mind as foggy as the distance that
my heavy eyes can barely see.

Tender-hearted nostalgia that
suddenly streams through my acing
body.

As I'm gasping for air.

I get a rush of acceptance, filling my
lungs with the richness of, air, for
one last time.

The eeriness of confusion doesn't feel
so bad anymore.

It is then, that I realize the mortality
of life.

One last glance into the fate that I
have been working towards.

Until I follow into the abyss."

– *Luca Gomes*

„You say you're sorry, but never what for.

Hurt is in the presence, love out the door.

Though my thoughts rest at ease.

My heart would shatter, my pain never leave.

Thy want happiness, I want peace."

– *Luca Gomes*

"Sometimes we are unsure if the relationships we engage in, will be profitable for us in the long run. We must make the decision, whether we are willing to stay and let the burning misery stay in our hearts until we somehow find a way to extinguish it OR do we take away the fuel that keeps the fire burning. That decision turns out to be quite difficult. A burning cellar can easily turn into a burning house. Love, in that sense, can be particularly difficult, especially when your house is on fire, and you feel like particular differences are too strong. Take a deep breath, take your time to reflect."

– *Luca Gomes*

„You once we're something I'd
adore.

Something I'd be proud of and
thankful for.

Now my vision has turned and my
picture of you has changed.

Our prior state, unable to regain.

I dedicate a poem to you, something
that is so precious to me.

Now all you did is making me leave.

I will not survive thinking of it.

All it does is, make me sick.

I get mad at you for so many reasons.

All you cared for is changing your
men, just like the seasons.

You've deceived me all the way
through.

So much that I don't know what to
do.

I told you I'd love you before.
That has gone out of the door.
All there is left is hatred nothing
more.

I can't be special, if half a dozen of
men has been before me.
I'm light on my feet.
My knees are too weak.
My bones begin to shatter but,
why would that matter?"

– *Luca Gomes*

„It's like going into a gold mine
without a torch – How will you see
the gold, when you can't even see
the light?"

– *Luca Gomes*

"When our gentle touches meet and
our lips collide, I get the feeling that
you have been touched before.
Like an unsold fruit that had been
laying in the tray for a while, you
have been picked up and put back a
couple of times.
You're covered in pressure marks;
you've got cuts and bruises. Every
time I take a bite of you, I can't help
but see the consequences of the utter
neglection that you have
experienced.

All I can imagine are all the different
hands that have touched you and
caressed your shell.

I get a foul taste in my mouth, while
my lips touch your shell and I try
biting into it. The fruit that once
was so enjoyable now is distasteful
and bitter. I cannot see you as the
beautiful and precious fruit that you
used to be. No amount of
imagination can change the taste that
you give out.

Irrationality. The 4th is the tenner of
a summer."

– *Luca Gomes*

„Each night I get confronted with
the empty side of my bed, that has
been vacated by your missing
presence. What if the emptiness is the
filler for my anger?
Could it be that I find enjoyment in
disparity?
Or could my disparity just be anger,
that results in my eerie emptiness?
In this very minute, I find myself in a
never-ending loophole that calls itself
overthinking. I shall deem my soul
with empty promises of a time that
has not yet risen, and I shall bleed my
soul to death by filling my emptiness
with events that will turn my
untroubled and joyous emotions into
a fatality."

– *Luca Gomes*

"I'm not tired of living.

I'm tired of not being dead."

– *Luca Gomes*

"The past is the informant of the present."

– *Luca Gomes*

„And when my mind gives in, to the reality that has not yet risen, it will then be, that my hollow feelings begin to fill themselves with sorrow."

– *Luca Gomes*

I often tend to create self fulfilling
prophecies because I think too much
about situations that haven't even
appeared yet. I overthink so much,
that I create every worst case scenario
in my head, leading to feel bad about
the situation and internal attribution.
I guess I need to learn to see all the
good possible outcomes instead of
just the bad ones.

"Love is a horrible feeling that makes you do irrational things, that will get you burned eventually because you invested too much of yourself and never even got half of it back. Take care of yourself."

– *Luca Gomes*

"It's the sheer ignorance of empathy or maybe even the lack thereof, that makes you wonder if you're even special to them in the first place."

– *Luca Gomes*

"It is the conflict between, do I stay with a person who's answers constantly make me feel bad and I'll try to get used to it, or do I run away and never try it in the first place?"

– *Luca Gomes*

"But what I know is that it rips me apart, so much, that I'm losing the lust in the daylight and the joy of the night-time."

– *Luca Gomes*

"My mind is a graveyard filled with
broken hopes and dreams,
sporadically visited by my hollow
thoughts and feelings, that struggle to
keep themselves afloat.
Soon after, when every little bit of
grief is used to heal from the scars
that I have put upon myself, my body
reliefs itself from every ache and
misery, turning my emotions into
grey, lifeless reactions."

– *Luca Gomes*

"Will it hurt more to leave?

Or will it hurt more to stay?

Certainty versus hope."

– *Luca Gomes*

"Do I fear the feeling of love, or do I fear what my mind has to say about it?"

– *Luca Gomes*

"It is when love and hate subside,
that you realize, the velocity of
emotions has decreased to a state of
vacancy."

– *Luca Gomes*

"They pulled me out of the dirt, thy put me into the dirt."

– *Luca Gomes*

"Lies are the expected scent of the wrong candle."

– *Luca Gomes*

Sometimes we allow people to persuade us with their lies, we let them make us think that they're something, that they really aren't. They paint this wrong picture in our heads about how they have acted in the past, but their actions show differently.
Can one be trusted thereafter?

Lies are just like a candle with the wrong label, you expect the scent that is written on it but get something completely different.

"You made me realize that people can lose their privilege to talk to me."

– *Luca Gomes*

"I don't want to talk any more, I really don't.

You say you'll be there for me, whenever.

But you really won't.

You'd stay with me through the weather.

Then I realized, you really don't."

– *Luca Gomes*

"You talk to me, when you want.
You make time for me, when you
want.
You care for me, when you want.
You look after me, when you want.
You say you care for me all the time,
but you don't.
You say you'll realize, but you
won't.
I will not give in, no I don't.
I will not let my foolishness take
over, no I won't.
I will stay true to myself, even when
you don't. "
– *Luca Gomes*

"I need to stop feeling like this
I need to stop caring so much
I need to stop doing so much
I need to stop giving so much
 Because nothing I do,
For my soul peace will ever be
enough."

– *Luca Gomes*

,,What if it hurts so much, that your tears don't even bother to tumble down your cheeks?

A once peaceful painting turned into shades of grey, by an artist that is so unknown, that the picture itself lost sense.

I never knew that such painting could ever scream at me the way it did.

Everybody's watching, that's what it feels like.

I once tried painting my own picture, seems like I've failed miserably. I used every possible shade of color, tried mixing them together as best I could. Gently I put together a painting on an empty canvas.. well, that's what I thought. It seems like

someone has touched it before and it
isn't in perfect condition anymore.
Sad to see my picture being ruined
by someone else's failed care.
My peaceful picture suddenly throws
paint back at me, not the one I used
on it though.
Seems like it's been scraping of
greyish paint from the one who used
to paint the canvas before me.
Colors of black and grey hit my face,
as I feel disgustingly violated and
mistreated by the effort I put in..
I desperately try to help and fix the
once so bright colors..
My brush gets pushed out of the light
touch I held it in.
Paint hits my face again.
I feel offended and hurt..

The artist who has been there before me, left me with a canvas, that I have tried to be gentle to, but hurts me, nonetheless.

How can it be that my gentle efforts turn into such drastic actions?

I have been the one trying to brighten up the canvas and give every little bit of love that I have left in me, to it. More than anyone else has done before me.. And what is left?

A two colored canvas that treats me the way it should have treated its artists prior to me.

That is just the way I see it though.. Again, everybody's watching. Why are they seeing a painting that differs from the one I'm seeing? They see the bright beautiful colors, that seem

to play with their eyes, it's like it
knows how playful it can be, using it
to get the attention it needs, or
maybe just thinks it needs.. or maybe
it doesn't even care at all and doesn't
think about it..
About what? About how it would
make me feel?
Pathetic.
There was a time where it told me,
that it would let me paint it again.
Oh how wrong I was for believing
that.. Eventually it kept asking for
different artists or artists it would get
gifts from, like new colors or brushes.
Aren't my colors bright enough?
Aren't my brushes soft enough?
Seems like I have used most of my
colors.. all there is left is black and

grey.. the only colors I never wanted

to use on that painting..

Eventually it used them on me"

– *Luca Gomes*

Page art and poems by *Luca Gomes*

About the author

Luca Gomes is a 23-year-old social work student from Germany. He acknowledged his poetic and somewhat philosophical side from an early age. In his original book of poetry, he describes his poems as a "safe place", "chaotic" and "therapy", which he uses as an outlet for his emotions felt at the time. This book is his first publishment and does not contain all of his poems that he has collected in his original book.

Credits and thanksgiving

First and foremost, I want to thank my girlfriend A. for motivating and mentoring me throughout the entire process of writing this book. I probably wouldn't have published this book, if it wasn't for her.

I want to thank my family for not giving up on me and always supporting my crazy ideas.

Lastly, I want to thank life for constantly giving me inspiration to write.

If you want to know more about me,

please visit my Instagram Page at

"chaoticmankindpoetry"